## This book belongs to:

..................................

 I read this book once!

 I read this book twice!

 I read this book three times!

Retold by Gaby Goldsack
Illustrated by Kim Blundell

Language consultants: Betty Root and Monica Hughes

This is a Parragon book
This edition published in 2006

Parragon
Queen Street House
4 Queen Street
BATH BA1 1HE, UK

ISBN 1-40548-704-6
Printed in China

# Chicken-Licken

p

# Notes for Parents

These **Gold Stars**® reading books encourage and support children who are learning to read.

## Starting to read

• Start by reading the book aloud to your child. Take time to talk about the pictures. They often give clues about the story. The easy-to-read speech bubbles provide an excellent 'joining-in' activity.

• Over time, try to read the same book several times. Gradually your child will want to read the book aloud with you. It helps to run your finger under the words as you say them.

• Occasionally, stop and encourage your child to continue reading aloud without you. Join in again when your child needs help. This is the next step towards helping your child become an independent reader.

• Finally, your child will be ready to read alone. Listen carefully and give plenty of praise. Remember to make reading an enjoyable experience.

## Using your stickers
Remember to use the **Gold Stars**® stickers at the front of the book as a reward for effort as well as achievement.

The fun colour stickers in the centre of the book and fold-out scene board at the back will help your child re-enact parts of the story, again and again.

## Remember these four stages:
- Read the story **to** your child.
- Read the story **with** your child.
- Encourage your child to read **to you**.
- Listen to your child read **alone**.

8

One day Chicken-Licken was in the
field when an acorn fell on her head.

"Oh dear!" said Chicken-Licken.
"The sky is falling in. I must tell the king."

Must tell
the king!

9

So Chicken-Licken went off to tell the king. On the way she met Cocky-Locky.

"Where are you going in such a hurry?" asked Cocky-Locky.

What's the hurry?

"The sky is falling in," said Chicken-Licken.
"I'm going to tell the king."

"I'm coming with you," said Cocky-Locky.

11

On the way Chicken-Licken and
Cocky-Locky met Ducky-Lucky.

"Where are you going in such a hurry?"
asked Ducky-Lucky.

Where are
you going?

"The sky is falling in," said Chicken-Licken. "We are going to tell the king."

"I'm coming with you," said Ducky-Lucky.

I'm coming too!

Must hurry!

On the way Chicken-Licken, Cocky-Locky and Ducky-Lucky met Goosey-Loosey.

"Where are you going in such a hurry?" asked Goosey-Loosey.

"The sky is falling in," said Chicken-Licken. "We are going to tell the king."

"I'm coming with you," said Goosey-Loosey.

15

They all walked on until they met Foxy-Loxy.
"Where are you going in such a hurry?"
asked Foxy-Loxy.

"The sky is falling in," said Chicken-Licken.

"We are going to tell the king."

"Ah," smiled Foxy-Loxy, who was a sly young fox. "You are going the wrong way. Follow me. I will show you the way."

So Chicken-Licken, Cocky-Locky, Ducky-Lucky and Goosey-Loosey followed Foxy-Loxy.

They walked on and on. At last
they came to a cave.
"Follow me," said Foxy-Loxy.
"This is a short cut."

But the cave was really
Foxy-Loxy's den.
Foxy-Loxy smiled as
Cocky-Locky, Ducky-Lucky
and Goosey-Loosey
followed her in.

Chicken-Licken was about to follow when

Cocky-Locky cried out loud, "Cock-a-doodle-doo!"

Cock-a-doodle-doo!

Chicken-Licken knew that something
was wrong.

She turned and ran away.
She ran and ran.

Chicken-Licken did not stop until she got
to the farmyard. Then she looked
around for her friends.

Chicken-Licken waited and waited but her friends did not come back.

Chicken-Licken knew she was a
very lucky hen.

I'm a very lucky hen!

Chicken-Licken never did tell the king that the sky was falling in. But the sky never was falling in, was it?

Chicken-Licken was a very silly hen!

But she never went near a fox again.

# Read and Say

How many of these words can you say?
The pictures will help you. Look back
in your book and see if you can
find the words in the story.

cave

acorn

Chicken-Licken

Cocky-Locky

Ducky-Lucky

field

Foxy-Loxy

Goosey-Loosey

hen

29